Sales-Driven Franchise Value

The Research Foundation of AIMR and Blackwell Series in Finance

Company Performance and Measures of Value Added
by Pamela P. Peterson, CFA and David R. Peterson

Controlling Misfit Risk in Multiple-Manager Investment Programs
by Jeffrey V. Bailey, CFA and David E. Tierney

Corporate Governance and Firm Performance
by Jonathan M. Karpoff, M. Wayne Marr, Jr., and Morris G. Danielson

Currency Management: Concepts and Practices
by Roger G. Clarke and Mark P. Kritzman, CFA

Earnings: Measurement, Disclosure, and the Impact on Equity Valuation
by D. Eric Hirst and Patrick E. Hopkins

Economic Foundations of Capital Market Returns
by Brian D. Singer, CFA and Kevin Terhaar, CFA

Emerging Stock Markets: Risk, Return, and Performance
by Christopher B. Barry, John W. Peavy III, CFA and Mauricio Rodriguez

Franchise Value and the Price/Earnings Ratio
by Martin L. Leibowitz and Stanley Kogelman

Global Asset Management and Performance Attribution
by Denis S. Karnosky and Brian D. Singer, CFA

Interest Rate and Currency Swaps: A Tutorial
by Keith C. Brown, CFA and Donald J. Smith

Interest Rate Modeling and the Risk Premiums in Interest Rate Swaps
by Robert Brooks, CFA

The International Equity Commitment
by Stephen A. Gorman, CFA

Investment Styles, Market Anomalies, and Global Stock Selection
by Richard O. Michaud

Managed Futures and Their Role in Investment Portfolios
by Don M. Chance, CFA

The Modern Role of Bond Covenants
by Ileen B. Malitz

Options and Futures: A Tutorial
by Roger G. Clarke

Sales-Driven Franchise Value
by Martin L. Leibowitz

The Welfare Effects of Soft Dollar Brokerage: Law and Economics
by Stephen M. Horan, CFA and D. Bruce Johnsen

Martin L. Leibowitz

Sales-Driven Franchise Value

The Research Foundation of
The Institute of Chartered Financial Analysts

Mission

The Research Foundation's mission is to identify, fund, and publish research that is relevant to the AIMR Global Body of Knowledge and useful for AIMR member investment practitioners and investors.

Foreword

To practicing security analysts and money managers, few things are of greater importance than the proper valuation of the stocks they hold in their portfolios. Although traditional tools such as the dividend discount model and price–earnings multiples have been (and remain) valuable weapons, today's rapidly shifting financial landscape often demands the use of sophisticated valuation methodologies capable of dissecting the sources of that change. One particular group of statistics that has drawn much recent interest is the so-called value-added performance measures, such as economic value added and market value added.

Despite receiving considerable attention in the past few years—see, for example, the recent Research Foundation monograph *Company Performance and Measures of Value Added* by Pamela P. Peterson, CFA, and David R. Peterson—these value-added metrics of performance actually have lengthy histories. In fact, the roots for both market value added and economic value added can be traced back about 100 years to Alfred Marshall's notion of economic profit, which is also the foundation for the net present value (NPV) technique widely used in capital-budgeting applications. The benefit to the analyst of adopting a value-added approach is that it allows him or her to focus on the ability of the managers of a company to increase shareholder value through prudent decision making (i.e., investment in positive NPV projects). Of course, the assumption implicit in all value-added measures is that the decisions that managers make—good or bad—will be accurately impounded in the firm's stock price.

Three years ago, the Research Foundation published a monograph that updated the standard price–earnings ratio approach to valuation within a value-added framework. Written by Martin L. Leibowitz and Stanley Kogelman, *Franchise Value and the Price/Earnings Ratio* is actually a compendium of several papers that the authors had produced at Salomon Brothers over a period of several years. In this monograph, they argued that a firm should be viewed in terms of both its current set of investment opportunities and its potential for investing in future projects that provide a return in excess of the firm's cost of capital.

The resulting model split the firm's observed P/E into two components: the base P/E and the franchise P/E. The base P/E is the reciprocal of the firm's market discount rate, and it reflects the set of investments presently in place. The franchise P/E is the P/E that the market assigns to the expected value of new and profitable business opportunities. By focusing their attention on this franchise factor, the authors argued that analysts could obtain a more accurate sense of how the market is valuing growth opportunities within a particular company. They also demonstrated that their model was robust with respect to such practical realities as inflation and taxes.

Leibowitz and Kogelman's concept has considerable merit, and it certainly has been well received within the analyst community. Although an earnings-based franchise factor is a compelling notion, it does suffer from some potential drawbacks. First, inasmuch as it resides at the bottom of an accounting statement, the earnings measure can be affected by myriad accounting interpretations on issues ranging from depreciation to goodwill. Second, earnings-based measures are challenging to interpret when evaluating multinational companies, or to reconcile when comparing a group of international firms subject to different accounting standards.

In this monograph, Leibowitz refines and extends his earlier thinking by basing the franchise-value measure on sales growth, thereby taking the notion of value added to the "top line" of the income statement for the first time. In addition to being a good deal easier to measure, the primary advantage of the sales-based approach is the specification of a franchise margin that accounts for the capital expended in pursuit of those new sales. It is this franchise margin, the author notes, that allows the analyst to assess the fragility of the "brand value" that a company may enjoy for a period of time; indeed, this statistic is perhaps the most important contribution to emerge from the present study.

As in his previous work, Leibowitz once again does an excellent job of providing the reader with a solid theoretical grounding for his unique way of looking at security analysis. In particular, he demonstrates how familiar concepts such as price–earnings, price–book, and price–sales ratios can be viewed within the franchise-value context. Through this effort, he makes a clear and lucid case for why companies must be viewed in terms of their ability to increase product sales and sustain their profit margins on those sales. As a result, he has added another important stepping stone in the path to understanding how value is created or destroyed. The Research Foundation is pleased to bring it to your attention.

Keith C. Brown, CFA

Preface

The work presented in this monograph represents the convergence of three different strands of events. The first is the earlier work on franchise value developed at Salomon Brothers in conjunction with Stanley Kogelman, which formed the basis for several articles published in the *Financial Analysts Journal* over the period 1990 to 1993. A more comprehensive treatment of this approach was then presented in the 1994 Research Foundation monograph, *Franchise Value and the Price/Earnings Ratio.*

The second strand arose out of a valuation model that was under development at CREF at the initiative of CREF's Director of Research, James Fleischmann. This valuation approach focused on the top-line sales and prospective sales growth of individual companies. The analytical technique was a "value added" approach that was strongly influenced by the writings of Alfred Rappaport.

The third event occurred when I was invited by Rosalie Wolf, the Treasurer of the Rockefeller Foundation, to participate in a special conference on international investment that was scheduled to take place in October 1996 at the Rockefeller Foundation's legendary villa in the town of Bellagio on Lake Como, Italy. Given the extraordinary setting, and the caliber and expertise of the fellow conferees, it was truly an invitation that could not be refused. My assignment was to discuss how the franchise-value approach could be applied to the special issues involved in international investing.

In beginning to think about this topic, it quickly became apparent that in a world dominated by large multinational firms, any one company's advantage of geographical locale, cheap labor, or more efficient production sites can always be replicated—in time—by a sufficiently strong competitor. Modern financial markets, with free-flowing and uniformly priced capital, exacerbate the difficulty for any firm to maintain an exclusive lock on being the low-cost producer. In the ultimate global environment, the key to a superior margin will be price, not cost. The high-value firms will be those that can command premium pricing across a range of product markets. Virtually by definition, such firms will be able to achieve higher-than-normal margins on a significant portion of their sales—in other words, they will possess a powerful sales-driven franchise.

Given this observation, a natural approach was to try to develop an analytical model based on the more "upstream" variables, such as sales and sales-related margins, rather than the traditional "downstream" figures of earnings or cash flow. Proceeding in this direction, we found that our earlier work on the franchise-value framework could be extended to incorporate Fleischmann's sales-based valuation models. The result of this integration is the current sales-driven model of franchise value. Even though the initial motivation was internationally oriented, the sales-driven franchise concept has applicability to many (if not most) domestic situations as well.

The basic ideas presented here are a natural extension of fundamental financial theory. A key concept that emerges is the notion of the "franchise margin"—the incremental margin on a given product beyond what could be realized by a new "commodity competitor" who would be content to just earn back the cost of capital. This gauge of a firm's pricing power reflects the true value of its product franchise.

In valuing any such source of excess returns, one central question is sustainability: How long can the franchise be extended and how severe will the impact be when serious competition finally arrives? This fundamental issue is often obscured in investment-based valuation models focused only on investment returns and earnings growth rates. In contrast, the sales-driven approach, by overtly focusing on sales levels and pricing effects, more naturally integrates an assessment of a franchise's "run" with its (generally inevitable) aging and decay. The sales-driven framework also helps underscore the importance of what we have called the "hyperfranchise value": a firm's potential for giving birth to fundamentally new franchise opportunities. This explicit treatment of franchise erosion—and franchise creation—is critical both to forming reasonable expectations of economic value as well as to framing appropriate consideration of risk scenarios.

Many of my colleagues and friends have contributed to the development and refinement of this work. Particular thanks must go to my former associate at Salomon Brothers, Stanley Kogelman, co-author of the earlier franchise-value papers, who provided an invaluable critical review of both the text and the mathematical exposition. My other frequent co-author, Lawrence Bader, also performed his usual careful reading with his inevitable good thoughts for improvements.

As noted earlier, the valuation models that were already under development at CREF formed much of the inspiration for this work. In addition to his role in this modeling effort, James Fleischmann deserves thanks for his many valuable observations and comments. For a heady combination of challenging reviews, probing discussions, and enthusiastic encouragement, I am greatly indebted to my analytical colleagues Eric Fisher, Paul Davis, Hans Erikson, and Russell Gregory-Allen. Several of my other associates at CREF also gave careful readings and useful suggestions that led to numerous points that found their way into this paper—with Carlton Martin, Leo Kamp, Brett Hammond, Jeffrey Siegel, Scott Evans, and Virgil Cumming deserving special mention.

Several other readers were very generous with their time and patience. Special thanks go to Peter L. Bernstein for his lucid critique and for being the first individual to cite these findings in a public talk. James Scott of Prudential Insurance provided a number of valuable comments. And a series of wide-ranging conversations with Jack L. Treynor led, as usual, to my having a deeper set of insights than those with which I began.

At the Research Foundation of the Institute of Chartered Financial Analysts, the Executive Director, Katrina F. Sherrerd, CFA, and the Research Director, Keith C. Brown, CFA, sacrificed several leisurely plane flights to reach a quick decision to move forward with this publication. I would like to thank them both for their speed and their decisiveness in bringing this document to fruition.

Any document of this nature entails a major effort to bring it into readable form. In this particular case, my assistant Mary Anne Prevost displayed patience, creativity, and precision in deciphering the many revisions that led up to the final manuscript. Without her special efforts, this monograph would simply not have seen the light of day. In a very real sense, she has been the hidden franchise behind this sales-driven franchise.

Others played key roles in the production process. David Paek helped to develop the Dow Jones graphs, and Leo Kamp helped with the other graphics.

I would also like to acknowledge the many valuable comments from fellow co-panelists at the Bellagio conference—Steven Ross, Antoine van Agtmael, Meir Statman, and Jack Meyer. And finally, a debt of gratitude is certainly due to Rosalie Wolf and the Rockefeller Foundation for having created the occasion, the gathering, and the magnificent setting that led to the further development of these concepts.

Martin L. Leibowitz
July 15, 1997

Sales-Driven Franchise Value

In a series of earlier papers, published together in 1994, Leibowitz and Kogelman developed a *franchise value* (FV) approach for estimating the intrinsic value of a firm's equity. Although derived from the standard formulations of the dividend discount model (Williams 1938; Miller and Modigliani 1961; Gordon 1962), the FV approach has the powerful advantage of being a more general (as well as more intuitive) formulation. This greater generality is helpful in adopting the FV model to today's global capital markets, where capital availability is often *not* the scarce resource (Bernstein 1956; Solnik 1996). Moreover, the FV model's focus on the price/earnings ratio (P/E) allows exploration of many facets of this key market variable—a variable that is widely used in practice but all too little studied from an analytical viewpoint. Even though the original FV development was based on the traditional earnings construct, it is an easy transformation to express the FV model in terms of net operating income, free cash flow, or other measures of economic value (Stewart 1991; Copeland, Koller, and Murrin 1994; Peterson and Peterson 1996). Because the earlier papers and much of current practice still follows the traditional earnings mode of analysis, this terminology will be retained here for purposes of consistency.

In this monograph, the purpose is to migrate from the return-on-investments FV model that formed the basis for the earlier work to a formulation that is based on the opportunity to generate sales—that is, a *sales-driven franchise value*. Although sales and investments are two sides of the same coin, it is a fairly major mental shift to view the opportunity for generating productive sales as the precursor and the ultimate motivation for investment (Rappaport 1986). This sales-driven context is especially productive in valuing multinational corporations. These firms have the size and reach to site production facilities anywhere in the world, resulting in a strong trend toward convergence in production efficiency. Increasingly, such megafirms are distinguished not by their production costs but by their distinctive approaches to specific markets. In other words, they create shareholder value though their sales-driven franchise.

The sales-driven FV model "looks through" the earnings to the more fundamental considerations of sales generated and net margins obtained. A key feature of the investment-driven FV approach is that it distinguishes between the current business and its future opportunities. In the sales-driven context, the net margin on the current level of sales is differentiated from the margin on new sales growth. This differentiation leads directly to the introduction of a simple, but powerful, concept—the franchise margin—to incorporate the capital costs required to generate these new sales.

The franchise margin has a number of important intuitive interpretations. First of all, it can be viewed as the present value added per dollar of annual sales. A second interpretation is that the franchise margin represents the excess profit that the company is able to extract from a given dollar of sales above and beyond that available to any well-financed, well-organized competitor who would be content to simply cover the cost of capital. This second interpretation can be especially relevant for a global market, where competitors with these characteristics are looming in the wings and would be able to field their products should any opportunity present itself. Moreover, in markets where cost-of-production efficiencies do not create any persistent benefits, the majority of the franchise margin will be derived from the company's ability to extract a better price per unit of sales. In such circumstances, the franchise margin becomes a good proxy for the *pricing power* of the firm's product in a given market. In this sense, the franchise margin truly represents the special value of a brand, a patent, a unique image, a protected distribution system, or some form of intellectual property that enables a company to extract an excess profit in a particular market (Treynor 1994; Smith and Parr 1994; Romer 1994).

One of the virtues of the sales-driven approach is that it shines a much brighter light on the fragility of a product franchise. In today's competitive environment, few products can count on long "franchise runs" with fully sustained profitability. At some point, the tariff barrier erodes, the patent expires, the distribution channel is penetrated, the competition is mobilized, or the fashions simply shift. Over time, virtually all products become vulnerable to commodity pricing by competitors who would be quite happy to earn only a marginal excess return. Even without direct visible competition, a firm may have to lower its pricing (and hence its margin) to blunt the implicit threat from phantom competitors (Statman 1984; Reilly 1997; Fisher 1996).

One way or another, the franchise runs out. When this occurs, sales may still continue to grow, but the margins earned must surely fall. Taken to the extreme, this margin compression will ultimately drive the franchise margin toward zero. And without a franchise margin, subsequent sales growth fails to add net present value and hence can have no further impact on the firm's valuation or its P/E. This effect can be surprisingly large—even for a highly robust franchise that lasts for many years. For instance, one example in this monograph shows how the prospective termination of a valuable franchise 20 years hence can pull a firm's current P/E from a lofty 22 down to less than 13. History has shown that franchise erosion of one form or another can spread beyond individual firms, sometimes with devastating effect on entire economic regions and their financial markets (Brown, Goetzmann, and Ross 1995). These fundamental issues of franchise limitations are much more clearly visible in a sales context than in the standard investment-based formulations with their emphasis on return on equity (ROE) estimation.

Another point of departure from Leibowitz and Kogelman is the focus on the price/sales ratio (P/S) as a particularly useful yardstick. As might be expected, the sales-driven orientation leads naturally to a greater role for the more "accounting neutral" P/S (Damodaran 1994; Fisher 1984; Barbee 1996). Moreover, P/S can sometimes supply better insights than P/E because of its more explicit treatment of any franchises embedded in the current business. Such franchises can have important implications for valuation and risk assessment, and they can also lead to a variety of paradoxical results. In a later section, an example is presented where an *improvement* in the current margin can *lower* a firm's P/E but at the same time *raise* its P/S. Thus, for a broad range of corporate situations, a variety of analytical and intuitional advantages favor the sales-driven approach relative to standard valuation methods and relative to the original investment-driven FV model. Exhibit 1 provides a summarized listing of these advantages.

With the sales-driven FV model, a firm's value depends on its ability (1) to sustain the pricing power required to achieve positive franchise margins on a significant portion of its sales and (2) to access new markets that can support a high level of sales growth. Thus, the sales-driven model emphasizes a corporation's ability to maintain an existing franchise, to create a new market for itself, or to successfully invade an established market. This competitive advantage in unearthing and attacking sizable markets distinguishes the highly valued firm that should trade at a high price/sales ratio (or a high price/earnings ratio). In a world with ample capital, with great fungibility of that capital, and with financial markets that can bring capital quickly to bear wherever excess returns are available, it is no longer the capital, the retention of earnings, or the financial strength per se that is the key ingredient of success. These are not the scarce resources in this new regime. The scarce resource is that special edge that enables a firm to extract franchise pricing for a product that is broadly demanded.

One word of caution is appropriate at the outset. In the application of any equity valuation model, the analyst comes to a crossroads where a fundamental decision must be made. Even a properly estimated valuation model can quantify only the current business activity and the more *visible* prospects for the future. In theory, all such visible and/or probable opportunities can be

3

Exhibit 1. Summary of Features of Sales-Driven Franchise Model

Retains Benefits of Investment-Driven
FV Model

Better Fit for Multinational Companies
Facing Global Equilibrium of
Production Costs

Sales/Margin Parameters More
Intuitive and More Directly Estimable
than ROE's

Places Market Opportunities as Central
Driver of Investment and Value
Creation

Relates New Market Opportunities to
Existing Sales Level

Underscores Role of Pricing Power

Segregates Product Margins from
Magnitude of Product Market

Clearly Distinguishes between Sales
Growth and Value Creation

Relates Sales Turnover and Capital
Costs to Franchise Opportunity

Explicitly Accommodates Competitive
Pressures on Future Margins

Clarifies the End Game Scenarios
Associated with the Termination of a
"Franchise Run"

Accommodates Phenomenon of Super-ROEs
from Rapid Leveraging of Prior
Investments into New Product Markets

incorporated in the valuation process. But any such analytical approach will fall short of capturing the full value represented by a dynamic, growing multinational corporation. Many facets of a vibrant organization—the proven ability to aggressively take advantage of previously unforeseen (and unforeseeable) opportunities, a determination to jettison or restructure deteriorating lines of business, a corporate culture that fosters productive innovation, and so forth—are difficult to fit into the confines of any precise model. At some point, the analyst must draw the line and define certain franchise opportunities as estimable and visible and relegate the remaining "hyperfranchise" possibilities to the realm of speculation and/or faith. To paraphrase Bernstein (1996), analyzing a firm's future is akin to assessing the value of a continually unfinished game in which the rules themselves drift on a tide of uncertainty. The purpose of this observation is to caution the analyst that the results of any equity valuation model should be viewed only as a first step in a truly comprehensive assessment of firm value. At the very most, the modeled result should be taken as delineating the region beyond which the analyst must rely on imagination and intuition.

Findings from the Franchise-Value Approach

Before turning to the development of the sales-driven formulation, recounting the basic findings from Leibowitz and Kogelman will be helpful. The FV approach provides a flexible approach to understanding how corporate and economic events affect the different components of firm value. Building on this foundation, we were able to develop new avenues of analysis for several important investment issues: reinvestment policy, capital structure, taxes, accounting practices, inflation, and equity duration.

These analyses led to the following observations, some rather surprising, about the determinants of the price/earnings ratio:

- A no-growth firm will have a low base P/E that is simply the reciprocal of the equity capitalization rate appropriate to the firm's risk class.
- The return from new investments should be differentiated from the current ROE—that is, new investments may have a different (and generally higher) ROE than the existing book of business. This differentiation is crucial because most firms have wide flexibility in their choice of new projects and can thus achieve future returns well in excess of their current ROEs.
- High P/Es result only when growth comes from new projects that provide sustainable above-market returns. Growth per se is not viewed as evidence of highly profitable investments. Only franchise growth contributes to shareholder value.
- In contrast to the standard models that assume a smooth and constant rate of growth, in the FV model, earnings growth can follow any pattern over time—no matter how erratic. The dynamic character of the modern business scene is grossly inconsistent with the notion of smooth growth. In particular, the path of franchise growth—the only kind that counts—is continually beset by competitive forces and hence is virtually never smooth.
- In the FV approach, productive new opportunities are assumed to be the scarce resource, rather than the available financing levels derived from retained earnings. Indeed, the level of retained earnings may have little

5

to do with the excess profit potential of new investments. If good projects are not available, earnings retention cannot create them.

- The P/E impact of new investments depends on the size of those investments relative to current book equity. Consequently, enormous dollar investments may be necessary to significantly affect the P/E of large companies.

- One particularly surprising finding is the effect of leverage. It turns out that increased leverage does *not* have a well-defined directional effect on the P/E. Higher leverage can drive the P/E up in some cases, or down in other situations. The key determinant of the P/E's directional sensitivity is the firm's preleverage P/E.

- High P/Es have an intrinsically fragile character. When franchise investment opportunities are limited in scope and timing, the P/E will decline toward the base P/E. To maintain a high P/E, a firm must continue to uncover new and previously unforeseen investment opportunities of ever-greater magnitude.

- Although it is commonly believed that price growth always matches earnings growth, this equality holds only under very special conditions. In general, as the firm "consumes" its franchise opportunities, the resulting P/E decline creates a gap between price growth and earnings growth. (The magnitude of this gap can be approximated by the rate of P/E decline.) Thus, one can have situations in which earnings continue to grow at a brisk pace but the price growth lags far behind—or even declines.

- The ability to pass along changing levels of inflation, even partially, can dramatically enhance a firm's P/E. A firm's future investments are likely to be far more adaptive to unexpected inflation than are its existing businesses. Consequently, when the value of a firm's equity is derived primarily from prospective businesses, its interest rate sensitivity (equity duration) is likely to be low. Thus, the FV approach helps explain why equities have much lower observed durations than the high levels suggested by the standard dividend discount model (DDM).

For the detailed analyses that led to the preceding results, the reader is referred to Leibowitz and Kogelman.

The Dividend Discount Model

In order to proceed with the main subject of this paper, it is necessary to first review the basic terminology and formulation of the standard DDM and the original investment-driven FV model. The standard DDM assumes that a firm's value is derived from a stream of dividends that grow—forever, in the simplest version—at a compound annual rate, g. Thus, for a discount rate, k, and a starting dividend, D (received one year hence), the firm's intrinsic value, P, can be written as

$$P = \sum_{t=1}^{\infty} \frac{D(1+g)^{t-1}}{(1+k)^t}$$
$$= \frac{D}{k-g}.$$

To relate this result to the current earnings, E, a retention ratio, b, is prescribed, so that $(1-b)$ becomes the payout ratio, and the preceding equation then becomes

$$P = \frac{(1-b)E}{k-g}$$

and

$$P/E = \frac{1-b}{k-g}.$$

When the further assumption is made that b remains fixed, then earnings and dividends must both grow at the same rate, g. Finally, with a constant ROE of r, this earnings growth is fueled by the earnings retention in each period:

$$\Delta E = r(b \times E)$$

or

$$g = \frac{\Delta E}{E}$$
$$= rb.$$

Example 1 illustrates how the basic DDM leads to a P/E of 13.89 for a firm that (1) has an ROE, r, equal to 18 percent on all current *and* future investments and (2) retains 44 percent of its earnings to finance its 8 percent annual growth rate. In this example, and throughout the monograph, the discount rate, k, is set at 12 percent. At first impression, this P/E of 13.89 appears rather low for such a high ROE. In point of fact, it is the high required retention rate of 44 percent that suppresses the P/E. To obtain a higher P/E, suppose that exactly the same growth rate of 8 percent could be sustained with a lower earnings retention—say 30 percent. Example 2 shows that this assumption does indeed

Example 1. Infinite Dividend Growth

Specifications	Standard DDM	Calculation
Infinite growth at compound rate $g = 8\%$, discounted by capital cost $k = 12\%$. Retention, b, is implicitly related to growth, g, and ROE $r = 18\%$, so that $$b = \frac{g}{r}$$ $$= \frac{0.08}{0.18}$$ $$= 44.44\%$$ Dividends are determined after retaining the fraction $b = 44.44\%$ of earnings to finance growth.	$$P/E = \frac{1-b}{k-g}$$ where b = retention fraction on earnings $(1-b)$ = fixed dividend payout k = cost of capital (discount rate) g = annual growth rate for dividends.	$$P/E = \frac{1-0.4444}{0.12-0.08}$$ $$= 13.89$$

Example 2. Same Dividend Growth as Example 1 but at a Higher ROE

Specifications	Standard DDM	Calculation
With ROE, r, set higher at 27%, the exact same $g = 8\%$ growth can be achieved simultaneously with lower retention, $$b = \frac{g}{r}$$ $$= \frac{0.08}{0.27}$$ $$= 29.63\%,$$ and hence with higher dividends and higher P/E.	$$P/E = \frac{1-b}{k-g}$$	$$P/E = \frac{1-0.2963}{0.12-0.08}$$ $$= 17.59$$

result in a somewhat higher P/E of 17.59, but it also implies a disproportionately greater ROE value of r equal to 27 percent. This example may appear somewhat counterintuitive because higher ROEs are typically associated with higher retention rates and hence higher growth rates. By keeping the growth fixed at 8 percent, however, one makes the tacit assumption that a definite limit exists to the opportunities for high ROE reinvestment.

These results derive from the intrinsic nature of the DDM. The simplicity of the basic DDM rests on the assumption of constant annual growth that is "self-financed" by a constant fraction of earnings retention. In turn, this assumption implies that a single ROE applies to both the existing book of business and to future investments. In moving to the investment-driven FV model, both of these conditions can be relaxed.

The Basic Franchise-Value Model

In its simplest form, the franchise-value model decomposes the intrinsic value, P, into two present value terms: (1) a tangible value (TV) derived from existing investments and (2) a FV associated with new investments, so that

$$P = TV + FV.$$

If E is the normalized earnings flow (i.e., the "perpetual equivalent") from the current book of business, and k is the discount rate, then

$$TV = \frac{E}{k}.$$

These earnings can be further factored into a product of the current (normalized) ROE, r, and the book value per share, B:

$$E = rB.$$

The second term, the franchise value, reflects the present value of all excess returns on future investments, with "excess" meaning the return above and beyond the cost of the required added capital. In other words, the FV term is simply the sum of the net present values of future projects. Under a wide range of conditions, this term can also be resolved into two factors. The first factor is the magnitude of new investments in present value terms, and the second factor reflects the average productivity of these new investments. To obtain the most basic representation, suppose each new investment dollar produces a stream of new earnings, R. To find the excess return, the annual cost, k, of each capital dollar must be deducted. Thus, the net stream of excess earnings available for today's shareholder (after compensating the provider of the new capital) will be

$$R - k,$$

and this stream will have a present value of

$$\frac{R - k}{k}.$$

The FV term thus becomes the product of the present value generated per new dollar invested multiplied by the present value (PV) of all such new investments:

$$FV = \left(\frac{R - k}{k}\right) PV_{\text{New investments}}.$$

9

With this present value formulation, one can move away from the simple growth models of the DDM and allow the investment process to follow virtually any pattern over time. A related point of departure is that the FV model allows for external and/or internal financing—that is, there is no requirement for self-financing limited by earnings retention.

To provide a more intuitive footing, a growth factor, G, can be defined that scales the new investments to the current book value:

$$G \equiv \frac{PV_{\text{New investments}}}{B}$$

so that

$$FV = \left(\frac{R-k}{k}\right) GB.$$

Therefore, the basic version of the FV model can now be written as

$$P = TV + FV$$

$$= \frac{E}{k} + \left(\frac{R-k}{k}\right) GB$$

or

$$P = \frac{rB}{k} + \left(\frac{R-k}{k}\right) GB,$$

where r and R represent returns on equity for the current and the new businesses, respectively.

In P/E terms, after division of the price by $E = rB$, the FV model becomes

$$P/E = \frac{1}{k} + \left(\frac{R-k}{rk}\right) G.$$

In Leibowitz and Kogelman, we found it convenient to define a franchise factor (FF):

$$FF \equiv \left(\frac{R-k}{rk}\right),$$

so that the P/E result took on the extraordinarily simple form

$$P/E = \frac{1}{k} + (FF \times G).$$

Thus, a firm's P/E is composed of a basic term—the reciprocal of the discount rate, which applies to all companies in the same risk class—and a second term that depends solely on the firm's ability to generate *productive* future growth.

As a simple example of the FV model, first consider the firm in Example 2 that turned out to have a P/E of 17.59 under the DDM. For the FV model in that case,

$$R = r$$
$$= 27\%,$$

so that the franchise factor becomes

$$FF = \frac{0.27 - 0.12}{(0.27)(0.12)}$$
$$= 4.63.$$

Moreover, for a set of investment opportunities that grow at an 8 percent rate, the growth factor, G, can be shown to correspond to

$$G = \frac{g}{k - g}$$
$$= \frac{0.08}{0.12 - 0.08}$$
$$= 2.00.$$

(This value, $G = 2$, also corresponds to an infinite variety of other future investment patterns that share the same present value when discounted at 12 percent. For example, a $G = 2$ also results from a 17.72 percent growth rate maintained for 10 years.) As shown in Example 3, when the FV model is applied to these values, we obtain the same P/E, 17.59, that was given by the DDM in Example 2. It is comforting to see that the FV model and the DDM always coincide when the firm specifications are the same.

In Example 4, the FV model's flexibility is used to specify two distinct ROEs—18 percent on the current book and 27 percent on prospective investments. Given that Example 4 has a lower ROE on its current investment, it may, at first, seem somewhat paradoxical that the resulting P/E, 22.22, is significantly higher than in the two preceding examples where both ROEs equaled 27 percent. In point of fact, as discussed earlier, the lower book ROE of r has no

Example 3. The Franchise-Value Model: Treating the DDM as a Special Case

Specifications	Investment-Driven FV Model	Calculation
The FV model segregates the P/E contribution into two terms: (1) the contribution from the current business, $$\frac{1}{k} = \frac{1}{0.12}$$ $$= 8.33,$$ and (2) the add-on from the franchise value associated with prospective new investments. This second FV term $(FF \times G)$ is itself composed of two factors that can be usefully separated: (1) a franchise factor (FF) depicting the P/E contribution from excess ROE on each dollar of new investments and (2) a growth factor, G, that relates the present value of new investment opportunities to the current book value.	$$P/E = \frac{1}{k} + (FF \times G)$$ $$FF = \frac{R-k}{rk},$$ where r = ROE on current book R = ROE on new investments G = present value of all prospective new investments with the ROE value of R depicted as a ratio to the current book value. For this example, both ROEs are set to coincide with Example 2, $$r = R$$ $$= 27\%.$$ For the special case of infinite growth at a rate g, $$G = \frac{g}{k-g}.$$	$$FF = \frac{0.27 - 0.12}{(0.27)(0.12)}$$ $$= 4.63$$ $$G = \frac{0.08}{0.12 - 0.08}$$ $$= 2.00$$ (Note that this implies that the PV magnitude of growth opportunities is "immediately equivalent" to twice the current book value.) $$P/E = \frac{1}{0.12} + (4.63 \times 2.00)$$ $$= 8.33 + 9.26$$ $$= 17.59$$ Thus, when the FV model is applied to the preceding numerical example, the resulting P/E coincides with that given by the DDM.

impact on the first term while it augments the P/E contribution of future investments because it falls in the denominator of the franchise factor,

$$FF = \frac{R-k}{rk}.$$

In general, a lower ROE in the current business, all else being equal, will always augment the overall P/E.

The Sales-Driven Franchise Model

A franchise opportunity may be derived from a well-defined ROE obtained through regulatory fiat or through the purchase of financial market investments. In such cases, the estimate of ROE is the critical variable, and the investment-driven FV model would be the most appropriate approach. In many other situations, however, the impetus for new strategic initiatives arises from the prospect of an exceptional sales opportunity. If these opportunities

Example 4. Higher P/E from Differentiating between ROEs on New versus Old Investments

Specifications	Investment-Driven FV Model	Calculations
One advantage of the FV model is that the two ROEs are naturally segregated. In this example, ROE on new business is kept at $R = 27\%$, but the ROE on the current business is lowered to $r = 18\%$. This reduction in r actually leads to a higher P/E. This result follows from the P/E contribution $1/k$ of the current business being independent of r.	$P/E = \dfrac{1}{k} + (FF \times G)$ $FF = \dfrac{R-k}{rk}$	Same as Example 3 in all respects except r is reduced from 27% to 18%. $FF = \dfrac{0.27 - 0.12}{(0.18)(0.12)}$ $= 6.944$ $G = 2.00$ $P/E = \dfrac{1}{0.12} + (6.944 \times 2.00)$ $= 8.33 + 13.89$ $= 22.22$

truly add economic value, then the capital investment involved in their pursuit should naturally lead to a correspondingly high ROE. But because the sales potential itself is the fundamental source of these corporate initiatives, using a sales-driven framework is generally more natural for estimating their impact on the firm's profitability, growth, and economic value.

In moving to a FV model based on sales, earnings are viewed as being the result of a given level of sales activity and a net margin that relates each dollar of sales to a dollar of earnings. For the current book of business, the annual sales, S, now becomes analogous to the normalized earnings stream, E. With a net margin of m,

$$E = mS,$$

and the tangible value of the current business can be directly written as

$$TV = \frac{E}{k}$$

$$= \frac{mS}{k}.$$

To provide an intuition regarding the magnitude of the net margin, m, Figure 1 plots the average net margin for the 30 stocks in the Dow Jones Industrial Average (DJIA) during the 1992–96 period.

The franchise-value term can be transformed in a similar fashion. Suppose the firm's future products and market developments are expected to lead to a certain volume of new sales in the future—above and beyond the current annual level, S. For simplicity, all of these new sales can be characterized as being

13

Figure 1. Average Net Margin of the 30 Stocks in the Dow Jones Industrial Average, 1992–96

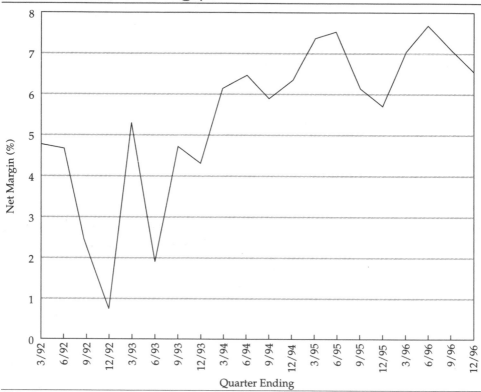

Note: Average net margin is calculated as the ratio of net income (before extraordinary items) to sales.

equivalent (in present value terms) to an incremental annual rate, S'. Then, S'/k will correspond to the present value of all new sales. If each dollar of new sales earns a net margin, m', then $m'S'$ will be the equivalent annual earnings associated with this new sales activity. But even in this sales-driven context, one must recognize that incremental sales require incremental investments in the form of capital expenditures and increased working capital. The need to pay for the additional capital detracts from the value of the new sales for today's shareholders. Assuming that a certain fraction, c', of each dollar of new sales must be set aside to cover the cost of this capital requirement, then the annual net excess earnings to today's shareholders becomes

$$m'S' - c'S'.$$

The capitalized value of this excess earnings stream corresponds to the franchise-value term in this sales-driven context:

$$FV = \frac{m'S' - c'S'}{k}$$

$$= \frac{S'}{k}(m' - c') .$$

The total sales-driven firm value then becomes

$$P = TV + FV$$

$$= \frac{mS}{k} + \frac{S'}{k}(m' - c')$$

$$= S\left[\frac{m}{k} + \frac{S'(m' - c')}{Sk}\right] .$$

If a sales growth factor, G', is now defined to be the ratio of incremental new sales, S', to the current sales, S,

$$G' \equiv \frac{S'}{S}$$

$$= \frac{PV_{\text{New sales}}}{PV_{\text{Current sales}}} ,$$

then

$$P = S\left[\frac{m}{k} + \frac{(m' - c')}{k}G'\right] .$$

The Franchise Margin

The capital cost, c', per dollar of sales is related to the commonly used ratios of sales turnover and asset turnover. For the purposes of this monograph, the term "sales turnover" refers to the total capital base that supports each category of annual sales. From this vantage point, the total capital base would include—in addition to inventory investment—all other elements of embedded or incremental capital. Thus, for the current annual level of sales, S, the turnover, T, would be defined as

$$T \equiv \frac{S}{B} ,$$

where B is the book value of the (unlevered) firm. Similarly, for the new sales,

S', the relevant capital base would incorporate expenditures for product development, added inventory, new working capital, new production and distribution facilities, the marketing launch, and so forth. The turnover, T', measure for these new sales would then become

$$T' \equiv \frac{S'}{\text{Incremental capital base}} \cdot$$

Because capital expenditures are assumed to bear an annual charge of k,

$k(\text{Incremental capital base})$

is the *annual* cost of providing the capital required to support the *annual* sales, S'. The capital cost, c', per dollar of new sales would therefore become

$$c' = \frac{k(\text{Incremental capital base})}{S'}$$

or

$$c' = \frac{k}{T'} \cdot$$

A similar relationship holds for the capital costs associated with the current level of sales.

Figure 2 displays a five-year history of the average sales/book value ratio, T, for the companies included in the DJIA. This graph is surprising because of the stability of these quarterly values around the average turnover value of 3.34. This remarkable stability is somewhat of an artifice in that it obscures significant company-to-company variation. For most of the firms in the DJIA, however, the company-specific turnover ratios appear to be fairly stable through time.

Returning to the theoretical model, Figure 3 plots the relationship of c' to the turnover, T' :

$$c' = \frac{k}{T'} \cdot$$

Clearly, as the turnover, T' , goes up, the cost of capital, c' , goes down. For a net margin, m' equal to 9 percent, a sufficiently high turnover (above T' equals 1.33 in the figure) is needed for the cost of capital to fall below the profit margin and lead to a true net excess profit. For a given turnover level, the extent by which the profit margin exceeds the unit cost of capital can be termed the "franchise margin", $(fm)'$:

Figure 2. Average Sales Turnover of the 30 Stocks in the Dow Jones Industrial Average, 1992–96

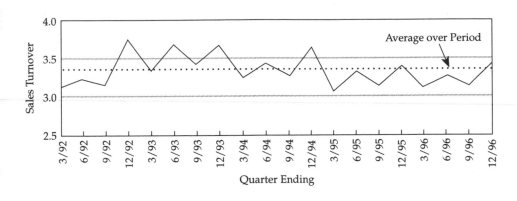

Note: Average sales turnover is calculated as the ratio of annualized sales to initial book value (based on index composition as of April 1, 1997).

$$(fm)' \equiv m' - c'$$

$$= m' - \frac{k}{T'} .$$

The basic valuation equation can now be written using this franchise margin as the coefficient for the net present value contribution of future sales:

$$P = S \left[\frac{m}{k} + \frac{(fm)'}{k} G' \right]$$

or

$$P/S = \frac{m}{k} + \frac{(fm)'}{k} G' .$$

Similarly, the franchise margin allows the P/E to be expressed quite simply:

$$P/E = \frac{P}{mS}$$

$$= \frac{1}{k} + \frac{(fm)'}{mk} G' .$$

Figure 3. The Franchise Margin: Annual Capital Cost as a Percentage of Sales, c', versus Sales Turnover Rate, T'

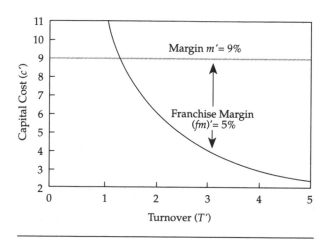

As an illustration of the sales-driven FV model, Example 5 addresses a firm whose characteristics are identical to the company in Example 4. With sales turnover ratios of T equals T', which equal 3, and with margins of m equal to 6 percent for the current book and m' equal to 9 percent for the new sales, one can see that the corresponding ROEs are the same as in Example 4:

$$r = mT$$
$$= 6\% \times 3$$
$$= 18\%;$$

$$R = m'T'$$
$$= 9\% \times 3$$
$$= 27\%.$$

In Example 5, sales grow at the same 8 percent rate that was used in the preceding examples for the growth of new investment opportunities. With this identical mapping of values, it is no surprise that the sales-driven FV in Example 5 produces the same P/E of 22.22 as the investment-driven FV model used in Example 4.

Example 5. Sales-Driven FV Model Coincides with Investment-Driven FV Model for Basic Situations

Specifications	Sales-Driven FV Model	Calculation
With the focus on sales and new sales opportunities, the two factors determining the franchise value now become: (1) G', a sales growth factor that relates the PV of future sales to current sales, and (2) $$\frac{(fm)'}{mk},$$ the P/E contribution per unit of new sales growth.	$$P/E = \frac{1}{k} + \frac{(fm)'}{mk}G'$$ The franchise margin, $$(fm)' = m' - \frac{k}{T'},$$ represents the excess profit on future sales beyond that needed to cover the cost of capital, which becomes evident by viewing $1/T'$ as the dollars of new capital required to generate each dollar of new annual sales. Hence, k/T' becomes the annual capital cost to produce $1 of annual sales, and so	Same specifications as Example 4 but with the following implied values assigned to sales parameters: $m = 6\%$ $m' = 9\%$ $T = 3$ $T' = 3$ Note that the above values imply that $r = mT$ $= 18\%;$ $R = m'T'$ $= 27\%$
This second factor consists of m = net margin on existing sales m' = net margin on new sales, and $(fm)'$ = the franchise margin $$= m' - \frac{k}{T'},$$ where T' = turnover ratio of new sales dollars to capital required to generate the new sales level.	$$(fm)' = m - \frac{k}{T'}$$ represents the net excess profit per dollar of new sales. Because $$(fm)' = 0$$ reflects the minimum margin for a rational competitor, $(fm)'$ is a gauge of a firm's pricing power.	$$(fm)' = 0.09 - \frac{0.12}{3}$$ $= 0.05$ $G' = 2.00$ $$P/E = \frac{1}{k} + \frac{(fm)'}{mk}G'$$ $$= \frac{1}{0.12} + \left[\frac{0.05}{(0.06)(0.12)} \times 2.00\right]$$ $= 8.33 + (6.944 \times 2.00)$ $= 8.33 + 13.89$ $= 22.22.$ (Same result as Example 4.)
To relate this model to the preceding example, note that, in general, $r = mT,$ where T = turnover ratio for existing book of business, $R = m'T',$ and $$G' = \frac{T'}{T}G.$$ But in this special case $T = T'$ $G = G'$ $= 2.00.$		

The Franchise Margin for the Current Business

The concept of a franchise margin can also be extended to the firm's current business. The implicit annual capital cost of the current book equity, B, is

$$kB.$$

With current sales, S, and margin, m, the net value annually added by the current business is

$$mS - kB = S\left[m - k\left(\frac{B}{S}\right)\right]$$

$$= S\left[m - \frac{k}{(S/B)}\right]$$

$$= S\left[m - \frac{k}{T}\right],$$

where T is the turnover of total *current* sales to the book equity. If a franchise margin, *fm*, is defined for the current business,

$$fm \equiv m - \frac{k}{T},$$

then the capitalized net present value of the current business becomes

$$\frac{mS - kB}{k} = S\frac{fm}{k}.$$

The firm's tangible value is the value of the current business—that is, the book capital already in place together with the *net* present value of earnings from the book investments. Thus,

$$TV = B + S\frac{fm}{k}.$$

With these definitions, the firm's value can be expressed in a more symmetric form:

$$P = TV + FV$$

$$= B + \frac{S}{k}\left[fm + (fm)' \ G'\right].$$

In this form, it becomes clear that the firm can exceed its book value only by attaining franchise margins on its current and/or its future sales.

The above expression for the tangible value is clearly too simple to address many of the dynamic changes that affect the existing business of real firms. Although many of these considerations could be handled through the appropriate "normalization" of earnings, sales, and margins, it is probably worthwhile to cite two explicit revisions that are often needed in assessing modern companies: (1) the impact of margin improvement, or deterioration, and (2) the need for continuing capital expenditures in order to maintain even the current level of sales.

First, in recent years, many firms have been able to maintain significant growth of earnings in the face of a very modest growth in sales. This result has been achieved by marked improvements in the net margin, often effected through major restructurings. For such situations in which further margin improvement or compression is believed to be imminent, an adjustment term may be required to capture the impact of the projected changes.

The second issue relates to the capital expenditures required to maintain the current level of sales. This issue obviously becomes entangled with the definition of net margin. Theoretically, to the extent that net margin actually reflects the earnings contributions, depreciation would already have been deducted. If a capital expenditure equal to this depreciation were able to fully maintain the current sales level, then no adjustment would be necessary. But in general, a greater or lesser capital expenditure is called for, and explicitly bringing this issue to the fore by adding another term to the tangible value component is often worthwhile. Such adjustments may be particularly appropriate in those durable-product sectors that require heavy capital expenditures to develop the new product models necessary to maintain even the current level of revenue. In such cases, large capital reserves may be present as part of the commitment to undertake such mandatory product development. These capital reserves should be recognized as having been essentially committed to internal needs and hence not available for ultimate distribution to shareholders. By the same token, appropriate added value should be recognized for situations in which the depreciation runs far in excess of the capital required to maintain the annual sales at the normalized level. With the appropriate interpretations of terms, the franchise-value model should be able to accommodate all of these situations.

Up to this point, the assumption has been that all sales from the current book of business can be represented by a single number and that all future growth can be related in some consistent fashion to this current sales level. But breaking down current and future sales in terms of identifiable product lines and geographical areas of opportunity is far more productive and insightful. In particular, one cannot begin to truly understand the character of a multinational company without examining its sales by geographical region. A product that may have reached maturity and has no further franchise margin in one area (often the home country) may have significant franchise margin and be a great source of value in other regions of the world. Such a product-line model represents a simple extension of the basic model.

Price Ratios

The preceding development focused primarily on the direct estimation of a firm's intrinsic value. In practice, however, many (if not most) analytical procedures are conducted on the basis of one or more comparative ratios. The field of financial analysis uses ratios of all types—from price/earnings to innumerable accounting measures. This almost compulsive drive for "ratio-izing" is motivated by several objectives. First is the understandable desire to achieve some relative comparability by normalizing for the huge differences in firm size. A second objective is to create some consistent gauge of value.

In the analyses of firm valuation, one often encounters ratios of price/earnings, price/cash flow, price/book, and sometimes price/sales. In market practice, the price/earnings ratio is clearly the dominant yardstick—and by a wide margin, although cash flow is finding increased use. But both earnings and cash flow are less than totally satisfactory because of their instability and the difficulty in developing broadly accepted "normalized" estimates (Treynor 1972; Fairfield 1994). Because many historical artifices affect book value, the price/book ratio also raises many questions as a basis for comparing firms. A firm's sales have a reasonable claim to being a good denominator in that sales are based on a fairly concrete flow that is affected relatively little by differing accounting conventions. It is, therefore, worth pondering why the price/sales ratio is so rarely used and the more volatile price/earnings ratio is ubiquitous.

The answer may lie with the second objective for forming these ratios: a gauge of value. After all, if earnings (or cash flow by some appropriate definition) is the ultimate source of equity value, then the analyst will want to know how much is being paid for a dollar of earnings. A related argument can be seen from the following basic relationships:

$$P/E = \left(\frac{1}{r}\right)(P/B)$$

$$P/E = \left(\frac{1}{m}\right)(P/S).$$

In other words, price/book and price/sales are less complete measures because additional variables—the ROE and the net margin, respectively—are needed to reach the "ultimate" price/earnings ratio.

Another, and more subtle, argument may be that the P/E level conveys information about a stock's risk level. This line of reasoning would suggest that a stock with a low P/E has a price that is supportable by the very concrete measure of current earnings. To the extent that the P/E rises above this level, it must be based on the more intangible (and hence more risky) prospect of future earnings growth. The FV approach, with its separation of "current" TV from future FV, accommodates the spirit of this interpretation.

When attempting to estimate a firm's value, the ultimate ratio is always the market price, $\hat{P}$, to the estimated intrinsic value, P. And any ratio that supports this goal is equally good. For example, if the analyst prefers to frame the intrinsic value calculation in terms of price/book, then the ultimate measure of market overvaluation will simply be

$$\hat{P}/P = \frac{(\hat{P}/B)}{(P/B)}.$$

Thus, in this context, the numeraire that should be used is the one that is most convenient to use, and this choice may obviously differ from analyst to analyst and from firm to firm. In this spirit of analytical convenience, the price/sales ratio may be deserving of wider acceptance. The virtue of sales as a relatively stable and "accounting-clean" measure has already been cited. Another argument derives from the thrust of this monograph. To the extent that assessing the firm's future franchise value is a critical element in the analysis, these projections may be more reliably developed in terms of future sales opportunities and the associated pricing power (i.e., franchise margins). In such cases, the price/sales ratio given by

$$P/S = \frac{1}{S}\left\{B + \frac{S}{k}\left[fm + (fm)' \, G'\right]\right\}$$

$$= \frac{1}{T} + \frac{fm}{k} + \frac{(fm)'}{k} \, G'$$

is a clear and compelling statement of the sources of value.

Figure 4 illustrates the P/S for the current Dow Jones companies during the 1992–96 period. The horizontal line in the graph represents the reciprocal, $1/\bar{T}$, of the average turnover during this period ($\bar{T} = 3.34$). The P/S value beyond this line provides a crude measure of the contribution from the two franchise margin terms in the preceding equation.

For situations in which other price ratios are desired, these can readily be

23

Figure 4. Average Price/Sales of the 30 Stocks in the Dow Jones Industrial Average, 1992–96

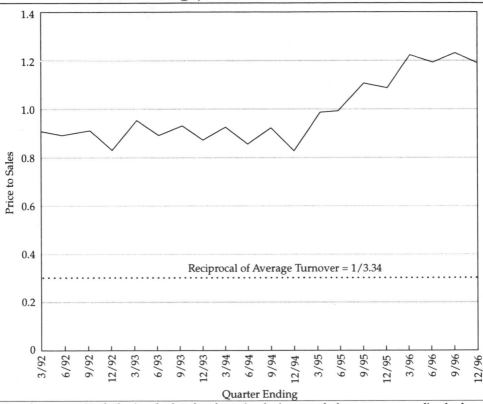

Note: Average price/sales is calculated as the ratio of price at end of quarter to annualized sales.

formulated within the sales-driven context. For example, the price/book ratio becomes

$$P/B = 1 + T \cdot \frac{fm}{k} + T \frac{(fm)'}{k} G' .$$

The P/E ratio can also be expressed in terms of the two franchise margins:

$$P/E = \frac{1}{mT} + \frac{fm}{mk} + \frac{(fm)'}{mk} G'$$

$$= \frac{1}{r} + \frac{fm}{mk} + \frac{(fm)'}{mk} G' .$$

But because the franchise margin on the current book does not play a necessary role in the P/E, it is generally simpler to use the equivalent form

$$P/E = \frac{1}{k} + \frac{(fm)'}{mk} G'.$$

Although all these ratios are theoretically equivalent in terms of the final valuation result, each ratio does provide a somewhat different slant on the analytical process. To illustrate these differences, consider the firm depicted in Example 6. This company differs from Example 5 solely in having a higher current margin (m = 9 percent versus m = 6 percent for Example 5).

In comparing the two illustrations, the first surprise is that the margin improvement in Example 6 leads to a significantly *lower* P/E (17.59 versus 22.22 for Example 5). The second surprise is that this lower P/E is associated with a higher P/S (1.58 versus 1.33 for Example 5, as calculated in Example 6).

The story behind this seeming paradox can be gleaned by observing that in the P/S formulation,

$$P/S = \frac{1}{T} + \frac{fm}{k} + \frac{(fm)'}{k} G',$$

the tangible value component reflects the franchise value provided by the current business. A larger current margin positively affects the P/S through its role in the *fm* term. In contrast, with P/E,

$$P/E = \frac{1}{k} + \frac{(fm)'}{mk} G',$$

the P/E contribution from the tangible value, $1/k$, is always the same, regardless of whether or not the current business generates a franchise return. Moreover, a higher current margin, m, will actually depress the franchise-value term because of its presence in the denominator. Thus, a higher margin, m, will always lead to a higher P/S but to a lower or equal P/E.

This problem with the price/earnings ratio's treatment of the current franchise margin is most dramatically exhibited in firms that have no *future* franchise value. All such firms will have a P/E equal to 8.33, but their P/B and P/S will appropriately vary with the magnitude of the current franchise. When *all* franchises are eliminated—both current and future—then all three ratios will fall to their respective base values:

$$P/E = \frac{1}{k}$$

$$= 1.33,$$

$$P/B = 1, \text{ and}$$

$$P/S = 0.33.$$

25

Example 6. Margin Improvement Can Simultaneously Lead to Lower P/E but Higher P/S

Specifications	Sales-Driven FV Model	Calculation
The P/E tends to obscure the role of any franchise embedded in the current business. This effect can lead to the paradoxical result that *higher* current margins (and hence *higher* current ROEs) can lead to *lower* P/Es. This effect was evident in Examples 3 and 4. In Example 4, r = 18% and gave a P/E of 22.22, but r = 27% in Example 3 and led to a lower P/E of 17.59. The price/sales ratio behaves more "reasonably"—that is, the P/S increases with improvements in the current margin and in the ROE associated with the current business.	The P/E reflects higher current margin only in the denominator of the future sales term: $$P/E = \frac{1}{k} + \frac{(fm)'}{mk}G'.$$ But the P/S provides recognition of a franchise margin in existing sales, $$P/S = \frac{1}{T} + \frac{fm}{k} + \frac{(fm)'}{k}G'.$$	In Example 5, P/E = 22.22, and m = 6%, so that $$P/S = m(P/E)$$ $$= 0.06 \times 22.22$$ $$= 1.33.$$ Now, if we change the current margin, m, to 9%, so that $$m = m'$$ $$= 9\%,$$ $$fm = (fm)'$$ $$= 0.05,$$ P/E is *lowered*, $$P/E = 8.33 + \left[\frac{0.05}{(0.09)(0.12)} \times 2.00\right]$$ $$= 8.33 + (4.63 \times 2.00)$$ $$= 17.59,$$ but P/S is *raised* $$P/S = m(P/E)$$ $$= 0.09(17.59)$$ $$= 1.58.$$ The basis for this effect is apparent from the full P/S formula: $$P/S = \frac{1}{3} + \frac{0.05}{0.12} + \left(\frac{0.05}{0.12} \times 2.00\right)$$ $$= 0.333 + 0.417 + (0.417 \times 2.00)$$ $$= 1.58.$$ Note that because $$r = mT$$ $$= 0.09 \times 3$$ $$= 27\%,$$ this example is now also coincident with Example 3.

Because *all* franchises, including current franchises, are theoretically vulnerable to competition, this greater discriminating ability of P/B and P/S should definitely make them worthy of wider consideration.

Option Values and the Hyperfranchise

From a theoretical point of view, the franchise-value calculation should incorporate all prospects and probabilities for sales at a franchise margin.

Theoretically, in an ideally transparent market, the analyst would be able to peer into the future to uncover all forthcoming additions to the firm's present value.

As was shown in Leibowitz and Kogelman, however, when the valuation model is based on a finite set of franchise-value opportunities, the firm will ultimately chew through these opportunities in the course of time. Eventually, it will exhaust the prospects, and its P/E will decline to the base value of current earnings over the discount rate (or in our sales-driven model, to a P/S that is just equal to the reciprocal of the turnover rate). In order to achieve an elevated P/E or even to maintain it at levels above the base ratios, management must access additional "franchise surprises" that were not previously embedded in the market forecasts. Of course, these surprises could take the form of actualizations of the happier outcome of prospects that had previously been only discounted probabilities (as when a new drug is actually approved for clinical use by the Food and Drug Administration). But a more general construct is to recognize that firms with access to sizable markets on a franchise basis are likely to have an organization, a management culture, and a level of corporate energy that can lead to future franchise opportunities that are currently unimaginable. This "hyperfranchise value" can surpass any anticipation of specific market opportunities that may be on the horizon. It represents a positive wild card in the valuation of a great corporation. By the same token, the cult of ever-growing market share and management ego trips can lead to destruction of value and may thus represent a negative form of hyperfranchise.

The hyperfranchise is clearly an elusive concept and generally quite difficult to measure. Nevertheless, it can be a major component of firm value. Many very practical business leaders focus on enhancing their firm's position to take advantage of potential future opportunities that are currently indefinable. To be sure, they do not call it "the pursuit of hyperfranchise"—"vision" is a more likely term. In some respects, it is like a game of chess in which a player may strive to achieve a positional advantage. And just as a chess player may sacrifice some tactical advantage to attain the better position, so a visionary manager may invest capital or even exchange visible franchise value in order to enhance the firm's hyperfranchise. Indeed, although foregoing maximum profitability to gain market share can be based on a variety of short- and long-term considerations, the pursuit of hyperfranchise may well be one such motivation. Any hyperfranchise will, of course, be dependent on the nature of the market economy at that time. When more opportunities open up globally, when trade barriers fall, when the best firms can freely confront their peers on a fair playing field, then a hyperfranchise will have a much higher value. In periods of economic contraction, trade frictions, and increased regulation, one can see how the hyperfranchise value may not count for nearly as much, even in the very best of firms.

Another source of value is derived from the optional characteristics of the franchise opportunities themselves. If we could truly trace out, on an expectational basis, all the franchise markets potentially available to a given firm, then we might be tempted to take that expected value as the gauge of the firm's franchise value. But if uncertainty exists in the circumstances surrounding these markets, or the magnitude of their potential, we must recognize that a corporation has the freedom to choose to enter the good markets when they appear good and to abandon what had been good markets once they turn sour. A company can time the entry into new markets so as to achieve the maximum impact for its shareholders. All of these options that are available to corporate management enhance the franchise value above and beyond its expected value. Clearly, this option value will be greater in a world that is uncertain, highly variable, and dynamic—one that is reminiscent of the environment we face today.

One particular option that is available to all growing firms deserves special mention: the option to time investments relative to fluctuations in the cost of capital. The cost of capital may vary widely over time, even on a real basis. Now, suppose we view the corporation as having an inventory of franchise opportunities, each with an implied ROE, which may itself have some degree of sensitivity to the market cost of capital. At a given point in time, the firm would consider pursuing only those new opportunities whose implied ROEs exceeded the cost of capital. As the cost of capital declines, more potential projects would become available for productive pursuit (and vice versa when the real cost of capital rises). This observation has major implications for how the changing cost of capital affects firm value. Thus, a firm's total franchise value could be increased not simply by the lower discount rate associated with lower capital cost but also by the broader range of franchise opportunities that would then become productively available. The option to take advantage of such fluctuations in the cost of capital is an important add-on to the franchise value of a firm. This "franchise inventory" view leads to the strong implication that firms might have an even higher duration relative to real interest rates than suggested by earlier studies (Leibowitz et al. 1989).

Sales Growth Models

The estimate of future growth is clearly a central component of a firm's valuation. At the same time, the process of growth estimation is well known to be particularly error prone. What is not broadly appreciated, however, is that many of these problems derive from implicit assumptions that are buried deep within the common formulations of growth. As we shall see, the sales-driven approach helps to clarify many of these problems and to facilitate the selection of the most appropriate growth models.

For the simplest class of growth models, the starting assumption is that growth proceeds smoothly, at a constant rate per annum, and that this smooth growth continues indefinitely. With this infinite horizon, we encounter the condition that a finite solution is achieved only when the growth rate, g, falls below the discount rate, k. Table 1 illustrates the sales pattern associated with 8 percent infinite growth. For this very special case, the growth factor takes on a familiar form:

$$G' = \frac{g}{k - g}.$$

Table 1. Infinite Sales Growth

Years	Current Sales		New Sales		Equivalent New Sales*	
	Annual Level	Cumulative Present Value	Annual Level	Cumulative Present Value	Annual Level	Cumulative Present Value
1	1	0.89	0.08	0.06	2	1.79
2	1	1.69	0.17	0.18	2	3.38
3	1	2.40	0.26	0.35	2	4.80
4	1	3.04	0.36	0.55	2	6.07
5	1	3.60	0.47	0.79	2	7.20
10	1	5.65	1.16	2.31	2	11.30
15	1	6.81	2.17	4.05	2	13.62
20	1	7.47	3.66	5.79	2	14.94
25	1	7.84	5.85	7.39	2	15.69
30	1	8.06	9.06	8.82	2	16.11
35	1	8.17	12.69	9.82	2	16.35
40	1	8.24	19.11	10.92	2	16.49
Infinite horizon		8.33		16.67		16.67

Growth rate	= 8%.	*Equivalent new sales = constant annual new sales that has same present value = 16.67 as actual new sales pattern.
Growth horizon	= infinite years.	
Growth factor	= $\dfrac{PV_{\text{New sales}}}{PV_{\text{Current sales}}}$	
	= $\dfrac{16.67}{8.33}$	
	= 2.00.	

This formula makes it clear how a growth rate of 8 percent, discounted at 12 percent, leads to $G' = 2$.

As mentioned earlier, the sales growth factor is really quite general and can relate any form or pattern of growth to the current level of sales, including various situations in which the growth terminates after some prescribed span of time. The most common and simplest form of growth termination is depicted in Table 2. In this table, a base level of *current sales* is continued in perpetuity, but the growth of *new sales* terminates after a 20-year time period, as shown in the column labeled "Annual Level, Effective" (for reasons that will soon become apparent). The resulting sales growth factor is

Table 2. Terminating Growth with Sustained Margins

Year	Current Sales Annual Level	Current Sales Cumulative Present Value	New Sales Annual Level Actual	New Sales Annual Level Effective	New Sales Cumulative Present Value	Equivalent New Sales Annual Level	Equivalent New Sales Cumulative Present Value
1	1	0.89	0.08	0.08	0.06	1.03	0.91
2	1	1.69	0.17	0.17	0.18	1.03	1.74
3	1	2.40	0.26	0.26	0.35	1.03	2.47
4	1	3.04	0.36	0.36	0.55	1.03	3.13
5	1	3.60	0.47	0.47	0.79	1.03	3.71
10	1	5.65	1.16	1.16	2.31	1.03	5.82
15	1	6.81	2.17	2.17	4.05	1.03	7.02
20	1	7.47	3.66	3.66	5.79	1.03	7.69
25	1	7.84	5.85	3.66	7.01	1.03	8.07
30	1	8.06	9.06	3.66	7.70	1.03	8.30
35	1	8.17	12.69	3.66	8.10	1.03	8.42
40	1	8.24	19.11	3.66	8.32	1.03	8.49
Infinite horizon		8.33			8.58		8.58

Discount rate   = 12%.
Growth rate   = 8%.
Growth horizon = 20 years.

$$\text{Growth factor} = \frac{PV_{\text{New sales}}}{PV_{\text{Current sales}}}$$

$$= \frac{8.58}{8.33}$$

$$= 1.03 .$$

$$G'(20) = 1.03,$$

which is about half the factor of 2 for perpetual growth. In some ways, this decline of almost 50 percent is surprisingly large, especially after a full 20 years of constant growth *and* the perpetual continuance of the high sales level attained at the end of the 20-year growth period. In Example 7, this 20-year growth period is applied to a firm having the same specifications as in Example 5, with the result that the P/E declines from 22.22 to 15.48.

More generally, given sales growth that continues for N years and then stabilizes, the resulting sales growth factor, as derived in Appendix A, becomes

$$G'(N) = \left(\frac{g}{k-g}\right)\left[1 - \left(\frac{1+g}{1+k}\right)^N\right].$$

Table 3 provides a tabulation of $G'(N)$ values for various growth rates and growth periods.

It is worth noting that this simple termination model enables us to deal with growth rates that could be far in excess of the discount rate and still get finite growth factors and finite firm values. It is also worth noting that the growth factor, G', remains the fundamental variable. It does not matter what the growth rate is or over how many years it persists, as long as it leads to the same growth factor, G'. Any growth pattern that leads to a given growth factor, G', will have the same effect on the firm's value. In fact, one can go beyond a smooth annual growth rate to any irregular pattern of development. Any such pattern, no matter how bizarre, can be represented by an appropriate growth factor.

Example 7.   Finite Period of Sales Growth: 20 Years at 8 Percent

Specifications	Sales-Driven FV Model	Calculations
One common assumption is that uniform growth continues for a specified period but then reverts to a lower pace associated with the general market. Both DDM and FV models accommodate such "multiphase" growth patterns. The tacit assumption, however, is that prior productive investments are unaffected by the step-down in growth.	$P/E = \frac{1}{k} + \frac{(fm)'}{mk}G'(N)$ $$G'(N) = \left(\frac{g}{k-g}\right)\left[1 - \left(\frac{1+g}{1+k}\right)^N\right]$$ N = number of years of growth $G'(N)$ is tabulated in Table 3 for various values of g and N.	Same values as Example 5 except for lower G': $G'(20) = 1.03.$ From Table 2: $P/E = \frac{1}{k} + \frac{(fm)'}{mk}G'(20)$ $= \frac{1}{0.12} + (6.94 \times 1.03)$ $= 8.33 + 7.15$ $= 15.48.$ (Significantly lower P/E than in Example 5 with its infinite growth at 8%.)

Table 3.   Sales Growth Factors

Years of Growth	Growth Rate						
	6 Percent	8 Percent	10 Percent	12 Percent	14 Percent	16 Percent	18 Percent
1	0.05	0.07	0.09	0.11	0.13	0.14	0.16
2	0.10	0.14	0.18	0.21	0.25	0.29	0.33
3	0.15	0.21	0.26	0.32	0.38	0.44	0.51
4	0.20	0.27	0.35	0.43	0.51	0.60	0.70
5	0.24	0.33	0.43	0.54	0.65	0.77	0.89
10	0.42	0.61	0.82	1.07	1.36	1.68	2.06
15	0.56	0.84	1.18	1.61	2.13	2.77	3.56
20	0.67	1.03	1.51	2.14	2.97	4.07	5.52
25	0.75	1.19	1.81	2.68	3.90	5.62	8.06
30	0.81	1.32	2.09	3.21	4.90	7.46	11.36
Infinite horizon	1.00	2.00	5.00	—	—	—	—

Franchise Termination Models

Although the basic growth model presented earlier has the virtue of simplicity, there is a certain logical inconsistency in the idea that a franchise advantage can be maintained indefinitely. Just as nature abhors a vacuum, so the world of economics abhors a perpetual franchise. Competition in one form or another will eventually erode even the very best franchise.

A key problem arises from the common confusion of terminology in the phrase "sales growth." This term is often used to depict the growth in the annual *level* of sales as opposed to the *total dollar value* of sales accumulated through time. In estimating the total value of the firm, however, the latter meaning is clearly the relevant one—the total dollars of sales in present value terms that the firm achieves at margins in excess of the cost of new capital. Thus, in characterizing how a franchise winds down, the key analytical issue is how to model the changes in the franchise margins associated with the various components of sales. One approach for dealing with "franchise termination" is to assume that any further sales growth beyond the termination point carries no franchise margin whatsoever. Such sales will have no present value impact and can thus be disregarded in the analysis of firm valuation. Although sales growth may continue indefinitely, the analysis can then proceed as if all sales growth came to an absolute halt at the termination point.

Even with this general formulation of "growth only to the termination point," different ways still remain for the franchise termination to affect the annual sales level reached at the termination point. The selection of the most appropriate of these "franchise termination models" can have a major impact on any estimate of a firm's value. The following discussion presents three different termination models, each with increasing stringency in terms of the franchise margins retained beyond the termination horizon. As a mathematical convenience, all three termination models are analyzed by keeping the franchise margins, *fm* and *(fm)'*, fixed but reducing the prospective sales flows to which they apply. In effect, this leads to reduced estimates for productive future sales. In turn, these reduced sales flows are characterized by lower sales growth factors.

The first termination model treats all on-going sales—at the annual levels reached at the termination point—as retaining their respective franchise margins. For obvious reasons, this model is referred to as the "sustained margin" case. In this case, the productive sales flows exactly correspond to those that would result from growth coming to a halt at the termination point, with the then-achieved annual sales level being continued indefinitely. This "sustained margin" model coincides with the basic terminating growth situations displayed in Table 2. In this case, regardless of how the "actual" sales may continue to grow, the "effective annual sales"—that which carries a positive franchise margin—levels out at the 20-year franchise termination point. Thus, the reduced growth factors presented in Table 3 can be applied to any sustained margin situations having the indicated termination points and pretermination growth rates.

This basic approach of growth termination at some specified time horizon is widely seen throughout the investment literature. In fact, the investment-driven analog of this growth horizon model forms the basis for virtually all commonly used valuation formulas—including many of the popular multiphase DDMs. In investment terminology, the assumption here is that all investments made prior to the termination point continue to earn the same ROE on an annual basis—past the termination point and on to perpetuity.

A second, and vastly different, "end game" treatment arises more naturally from the sales-driven context. Suppose that franchise termination means that from the termination point forward, the margins collapse down to a commodity pricing level on *all* new sales growth (i.e., on all sales above the original level associated with the current book of business). This assumption is radically different in that it curtails all increments of value from any such "new-sales" beyond the termination point. In this "collapsing new margin" interpretation, the residual value for today's shareholders of future new sales beyond the termination point is zero! Intuitional clarity would seem to argue for this cruder, but simpler, model of a total cessation of value enhancement. After all, when a market ceases to provide franchise pricing, the margin collapse should logically apply to all such future sales. Just because a given level of new sales was reached prior to the termination point, it does not follow that this sales level should be spared from the margin collapse. As might be expected, a firm's estimated value may be radically reduced when an analyst shifts from a "sustained franchise" to a "collapsing new margin" viewpoint.

Example 8 addresses this issue by assuming that, after 20 years, all sales *above the original level* are subject to the margin squeeze. As noted earlier, the sales-driven FV calculation can proceed by keeping the franchise margins fixed but reducing the sales growth factor to account for only the productive sales flow under this franchise termination model. Within this framework, the termination condition is equivalent to having the total annual sales (i.e., the original sales plus the new sales) rise to 4.66 times the original level by the 20th year, and then suddenly drop back to 1.00 times the original level and remain there in perpetuity. Based on the analysis developed in Appendix B, Table 4 schematically depicts the pattern of productive sales (i.e., those with a positive franchise margin) generated by this "collapsing new margin" model. This reduced flow of sales naturally leads to a further decline in the sales growth factor to 0.69. The P/E also undergoes a significant drop to 13.12, dramatically illustrating the vulnerability of investment-driven models that tend to overlook these more powerful margin squeezes.

Table 5 provides a tabulation of growth factors for these first two termination models across a range of growth rates and termination horizons. As discussed earlier, the 8 percent growth terminating at 20 years can be seen to lead to growth factors of 1.03 with a sustained margin and to 0.69 with collapsing new margins. Note that these values represent only 52 percent and 35 percent, respectively, of

Example 8. Collapsing Margin on Newly Developed Sales after 20-Year Growth Period

Specifications	Sales-Driven FV Model	Calculation
Same growth pattern as in preceding examples, but after the 20th year, competitive pressures are assumed to drive the franchise margin to zero:	$P/E = \dfrac{1}{k} + \dfrac{(fm)'}{mk} G'(N)$	Same values as Example 7 except for even lower G' :
$(fm)' = 0.$	The collapsing margin situation is shown in Table 4 to result in a growth factor of $G'(20) = 0.69$. By focusing on the ability to sustain a franchise margin, the sales-driven FV model underscores the limits to a product franchise in today's competitive global market. This point is often overlooked in the standard multiphase models because it is all too easy to implicitly assume that all previous investments continue to earn the same high initial ROE forever.	$G'(20) = 0.69.$
For convenience, this competitive-margin effect is captured through a reduced sales growth factor. In fact, actual sales growth may continue beyond the 20th year, but with $(fm)' = 0$, there is no further contribution to firm value or to the P/E.		$P/E = \dfrac{1}{k} + \dfrac{(fm)'}{mk} G'(20)$ $= 8.33 + (6.94 \times 0.69)$ $= 8.33 + 4.79$ $= 13.12.$ (Significantly lower than the P/E of 15.48 achieved in Example 7.)

Table 4. Terminating Growth with Collapsing New Margins

Year	Current Sales		New Sales			Equivalent New Sales	
	Annual Level	Cumulative Present Value	Annual Level		Cumulative Present Value	Annual Level	Cumulative Present Value
			Actual	Effective			
1	1	0.89	0.08	0.08	0.06	0.69	0.62
2	1	1.69	0.17	0.17	0.18	0.69	1.17
3	1	2.40	0.26	0.26	0.35	0.69	1.66
4	1	3.04	0.36	0.36	0.55	0.69	2.10
5	1	3.60	0.47	0.47	0.79	0.69	2.49
10	1	5.65	1.16	1.16	2.31	0.69	3.90
15	1	6.81	2.17	2.17	4.05	0.69	4.70
20	1	7.47	3.66	3.66	5.79	0.69	5.15
25	1	7.84	5.85	0	5.79	0.69	5.41
30	1	8.06	9.06	0	5.79	0.69	5.56
35	1	8.17	12.69	0	5.79	0.69	5.64
40	1	8.24	19.11	0	5.79	0.69	5.69
Infinite horizon		8.33			5.79		5.79

Discount rate = 12%.
Growth rate = 8%.
Growth horizon = 20 years.

$$\text{Growth factor} = \frac{PV_{\text{New Sales}}}{PV_{\text{Current Sales}}}$$

$$= \frac{5.79}{8.33}$$

$$= 0.69.$$

the full growth factor of 2.00 that would result from perpetual growth at 8 percent. These are surprisingly significant reductions after a full 20 years of growth. From the third row of Table 5, it can be seen that with faster growth (10 percent) and a shorter termination horizon of 10 years, margin compression forces even more dramatic reductions—to 16 percent and 7 percent—relative to the perpetual growth factor of 5.00. These results underscore the need to confront the critical issue of franchise termination in every analysis of firm value.

The third, and most stringent, termination model assumes that all franchise margins collapse. In other words, this "total margin collapse" model presumes that if competition is so fierce as to drive the franchise margin on *new* sales down to zero, then it is also likely to destroy any franchise margin on *current* sales. (An exception to this argument might be multinational environments with differential barriers to competition.)

Table 5. Sales Growth Factors for Various Termination Models

Growth Rate	Growth Factor for Perpetual Growth with Sustained Margin	Number of Years Growth Before Termination	Sustained Margin		Collapsing New Margin		
			Terminated Growth Factor with Sustained Margin	As Percentage of Perpetual Growth with Sustained Margin	Terminated Growth Factor with Collapsing New Margin	As Percentage of Terminated Growth with Sustained Margin	As Percentage of Perpetual Growth with Sustained Margin
6%	1.00	10	0.42	42%	0.20	48%	20%
8	2.00	10	0.61	32	0.28	45	14
10	5.00	10	0.82	16	0.37	45	7
12	∞	10	1.07	—	0.47	44	—
14	∞	10	1.36	—	0.58	43	—
16	∞	10	1.68	—	0.70	42	—
18	∞	10	2.06	—	0.84	41	—
6	1.00	20	0.67	67	0.46	67	46
8	2.00	20	1.03	52	0.69	67	35
10	5.00	20	1.51	30	0.98	65	20
12	∞	20	2.14	—	1.34	63	—
14	∞	20	2.97	—	1.79	60	—
16	∞	20	4.07	—	2.36	58	—
18	∞	20	5.52	—	3.08	56	—
6	1.00	30	0.81	81	0.67	83	67
8	2.00	30	1.38	69	1.06	77	53
10	5.00	30	2.09	42	1.60	77	32
12	∞	30	3.21	—	2.35	73	—
14	∞	30	4.90	—	3.42	70	—
16	∞	30	7.46	—	4.93	66	—
18	∞	30	11.36	—	7.11	63	—

Example 9. Collapsing Margin on Total Sales after 20-Year Growth Period

Specifications	Sales-Driven FV Model	Calculations
Same situation as in Example 8 but with the added stringency that after 20 years, margins collapse to "commodity levels" on total sales—both existing sales and new sales; that is,	From Appendix C, $P/E = \dfrac{1}{mT} + \left(\dfrac{fm}{m}\right)\dfrac{1}{k}\left[1 - \left(\dfrac{1}{1+k}\right)^{N+1}\right]$ $+ \dfrac{(fm)'}{mk}G'(N)$	Because $\left[1 - \left(\dfrac{1}{1+k}\right)^{N+1}\right] = \left[1 - \left(\dfrac{1}{1.12}\right)^{21}\right]$ $= 0.91,$ we have
$fm = (fm)'$ $= 0.$		$P/E = \dfrac{1}{mT} + \left(\dfrac{fm}{m}\right)\dfrac{1}{k}(0.91) + \dfrac{(fm)'}{mk}G'(20)$
The effect of this "total margin collapse" is quite modest after 20 years, but it can have a much larger impact for shorter-growth periods.		$= \dfrac{1}{0.06 \times 3} + \left(\dfrac{0.02}{0.06}\right)\left(\dfrac{1}{0.12}\right)(0.91) + 6.94 \times 0.69$ $= 5.56 + 2.53 + 4.79$ $= 12.90.$

Example 9 demonstrates this ultimate level of competition in which the margin compression extends to all sales, including those derived from the firm's original book of business. The pattern of effective sales is shown in Table 6, with the detailed analysis provided in Appendix C. As might be expected, this curtailment of value lowers the first term in the FV model, leading to, in this case, a slightly lower P/E of 12.90 percent. This modest reduction is a direct result of the choice of a 20-year initial period; shorter horizons would result in a more serious decrement.

The preceding discussion of termination models is certainly not intended to be an exhaustive characterization of how franchises can wind down. Indeed, just as the creation and development of a franchise is a highly complex and dynamic process, so a franchise's expiration may take on far more forms than can be readily categorized. Rather, the purpose in exploring the implications of these three simple termination models is to illustrate the following key points:

- Virtually any limit to a firm's franchise (even after as long a run as 20 years) can have an extraordinary impact on firm value.
- Seemingly subtle differences in the assumed nature of the franchise limit can also lead to major valuation swings.
- The sales-driven model, by its very nature, brings to the surface these fundamental analytical issues that lie buried within the more standard investment-driven formulation.

Modeling Super-ROEs

In many situations, new business prospects arise that require only minimal capital investment. Typically, in these instances, the firm finds itself in a

Table 6. Terminating Growth with Total Margin Collapse

| | Current Sales | | | New Sales | | | Current New Sales | |
| | Annual Level | | | Annual Level | | | | |
Years	Actual	Effective	Cumulative Present Value	Actual	Effective	Cumulative Present Value	Annual Level	Cumulative Present Value
1	1	1	0.89	0.08	0.08	0.06	0.69	0.62
2	1	1	1.69	0.17	0.17	0.18	0.69	1.17
3	1	1	2.40	0.26	0.26	0.35	0.69	1.66
4	1	1	3.04	0.36	0.36	0.55	0.69	2.10
5	1	1	3.60	0.47	0.47	0.79	0.69	2.49
10	1	1	5.65	1.16	1.16	2.31	0.69	3.90
15	1	1	6.81	2.17	2.17	4.05	0.69	4.70
20	1	1	7.47	3.66	3.66	5.79	0.69	5.15
25	1	0	7.56	5.85	0	5.79	0.69	5.41
30	1	0	7.56	9.06	0	5.79	0.69	5.56
35	1	0	7.56	12.69	0	5.79	0.69	5.64
40	1	0	7.56	19.11	0	5.79	0.69	5.69
Infinite horizon			7.56[a]			5.79		5.79

[a]Following the growth/receipt convention explained in Appendix C, the current sales receipts bearing the full initial 6% margin would extend through the end of the 21st year (i.e., after 20 years of sales growth), resulting in a cumulative present value = 7.56.

Discount rate = 12%.
Growth rate = 8%.
Growth horizon = 20 years.

position to reap windfall sales, and profits, by leveraging off of its past investments in product development, manufacturing facilities, marketing campaigns, and/or distribution channels. The magnitude of the business opportunity can often be quite sizable, particularly in a global context where a firm with a strong brand-name product can penetrate major new markets with very modest capital expenditures. Because the required incremental investment is so small, and the reward can be so large, the ROEs on these prospects can be enormous. For managers, the ROE is rarely the question; they just move forward. But for the investment analyst, the prospect of these windfall opportunities may present a significant addition to firm value. In investment-driven models, making a reasoned estimate of ROE that may at first appear to be ridiculously high becomes difficult. A far more palatable approach is to estimate the size of the prospective new market and the obtainable margin—that is, to pursue the sales-driven route to evaluation.

Example 10 considers the same 20-year growth situation as Example 9. But in this case, only a minimal capital investment is required to realize this sales growth. This example goes to the extreme limit where the turnover, T', becomes virtually infinite, which drives the franchise margin, $(fm)'$, to coincide with the margin itself,

Example 10. Near-Infinite Turnovers and Super-ROEs from Leveraging Existing Investments

Specifications	Sales-Driven FV Model	Calculation
With new international markets opening up, many firms achieve enormous sales improvements with minimal new investments. The investment-driven models go awry with ROEs approaching these super-high levels. The sales-driven FV model, however, can readily handle these surprisingly not uncommon situations by using G' to directly capture the PV opportunity for new sales and by letting $$(fm)' = m' - \frac{k}{T'} \to m'$$ as the incremental turnover $T' \to \infty$. Essentially, the profits on these new sales represent a windfall to firm value because there is virtually no associated capital cost.	$$P/E = \frac{1}{mT} + \left(\frac{fm}{m}\right)\frac{1}{k}\left[1 - \left(\frac{1}{1+k}\right)^{N+1}\right]$$ $$+ \frac{m'}{mk}G'(N)$$	Same as Example 9 except $$(fm)' = m' - \frac{k}{T} \to m'$$ $$\frac{(fm)'}{mk} = \frac{m'}{mk}$$ $$= \frac{0.09}{(0.06)(0.12)}$$ $$= 12.50$$ $$P/E = 5.56 + 2.53 + \frac{m'}{mk}G'(20)$$ $$= 5.56 + 2.53 + (12.50 \times 0.69)$$ $$= 5.56 + 2.53 + 8.63$$ $$= 16.73$$ (Note significant escalation in P/E from Example 9.)

$$(fm)' = m'$$
$$= 0.09,$$

and leads to a significant escalation of the P/E to 16.73.

Conclusion

The sales-driven franchise value approach suggests a rather different way to view multinational firms. Suppose that one can envision the global economy in the future as being composed of a set of current product markets, new product markets, and even some hypothetical "hypermarkets" of the yet-to-be-imagined variety. One can then ask the question: "Which firms have the ability to access these markets in a fashion that will generate a positive franchise margin for a significant span of time?" The first set of candidates will be corporations with areas of regional dominance where the franchise is achieved by barriers to entry that can persist into the future (e.g., German life insurance companies may enjoy a particular competitive advantage for some time with respect to German nationals). In other cases, the brand name and associated imagery surrounding a particular product may carry its franchise far into the future. In all cases, one would be well advised to think of the inevitable pressures that must be brought to bear on positive franchise margins and to think about their likely duration in the face of global competition and new product innovation. Those firms that can lever their existing product line and corporate resources to deliver products that truly have pricing power (and the value added that justifies that pricing power) should be the long-term winners in this valuation game.

Appendix A: Derivation of the Constant-Growth Model

The concept of the sales growth factor implies that all future sales growth is equivalent (on a present value basis) to an instantaneous jump of S' to a new constant level of annual sales, where S' equals $G'S$ (Table 1). To explore the assumptions embedded in this growth model and its related forms, one must delve into the algebraic derivation of this result.

At the outset, the nature of the growth process must be precisely defined. The basic approach is to assume that a sales *rate* achieved at the beginning of the year leads to a sales *receipt* at the end of that same year. Thus, the original annual sales rate leads to receipts of S dollars at the end of the first year, S dollars at the end of the second year, and so forth. By the same principle, the sales growth at the rate g will be viewed as raising the level of annual sales to a *going-forward* rate of $(1 + g)S$ by the end of the first year. The incremental sales (gS) associated with this first year of sales growth will be received at the end of the second year, the third year, and so forth, producing a capitalized value two years hence of

$$gS\left[1 + \left(\frac{1}{1+k}\right) + \left(\frac{1}{1+k}\right)^2 + \dots\right]$$

$$= gS\left[\frac{1}{1 - \left(\frac{1}{1+k}\right)}\right]$$

$$= \frac{gS(1+k)}{k}$$

with a current present value of

$$\frac{1}{(1+k)^2}\frac{gS(1+k)}{k} = \frac{gS}{(1+k)k}.$$

The above expression thus represents the present value contribution of the first year's growth in the sales rate. Similarly, by the end of the second year, the new "going forward" incremental sales rate will be

$$g(1 + g)S,$$

which will produce a future income stream that, starting at the end of the third year, will have a *then*-present value of

$$\frac{g(1+g)S(1+k)}{k}.$$

By discounting this third-year value back to the present, we obtain

$$\frac{1}{(1+k)^3}\left[\frac{g(1+g)S(1+k)}{k}\right] = \frac{1}{(1+k)^2}\left[\frac{g(1+g)S}{k}\right].$$

In general, the present value contribution of the sales growth generated by the end of the year t will be

$$\frac{gS}{k(1+k)}\left(\frac{1+g}{1+k}\right)^{t-1}.$$

Suppose this growth process continues for N years and then, for some reason, comes to an abrupt halt, so that the annual sales rate remains fixed at the level reached at the end of year N. The annual sales would then follow the pattern depicted in Table 1. The preceding expression corresponds to the present value of new sales generated in year t. Consequently, the sum total of all such present values from the first year to year N will correspond to the present value of all incremental sales:

$$\frac{gS}{k(1+k)}\sum_{t=1}^{N}\left(\frac{1+g}{1+k}\right)^{t-1} = \frac{gS}{k(1+k)}\left[\frac{1-\left(\frac{1+g}{1+k}\right)^{N}}{1-\left(\frac{1+g}{1+k}\right)}\right]$$

$$= \left(\frac{gS}{k}\right)\frac{1}{k-g}\left[1-\left(\frac{1+g}{1+k}\right)^{N}\right].$$

By definition,

$$G' \equiv \frac{PV_{\text{Incremental new sales}}}{PV_{\text{Current sales}}}$$

$$= \frac{PV_{\text{Incremental new sales}}}{S/k}$$

$$= \frac{\left(\frac{gS}{k}\right)\frac{1}{k-g}\left[1-\left(\frac{1+g}{1+k}\right)^{N}\right]}{S/k}$$

$$= \left(\frac{g}{k-g}\right)\left[1-\left(\frac{1+g}{1+k}\right)^{N}\right].$$

The values of G' are tabulated in Table 3 for various growth rates, g, and time horizons, N.

For the important special case of perpetual growth, we must have k greater than g in order to obtain a finite growth factor:

$$G' = \frac{g}{k-g}.$$

Appendix B: New Margin Collapse Models

As developed in Appendix A, the first year's sales growth creates a payment stream, gS, that, if continued to perpetuity, will have a present value contribution of

$$\frac{gS}{(1+k)^2}\left[1+\left(\frac{1}{1+k}\right)+\left(\frac{1}{1+k}\right)^2+\ldots\right] = \frac{gS}{(1+k)k} .$$

On the other hand, if the margin collapses after year N, with

$$m' \to \frac{k}{T'}$$

and

$$(fm)' \to 0,$$

then all future sales beyond the year $(N+1)$ will have absolutely no impact on the firm's valuation. Thus, from the valuation viewpoint, it is equivalent to having the sales stream come to an abrupt halt. In essence, the payment tail after year $(N+1)$ is being dropped, thereby changing the present value to

$$\frac{gS}{(1+k)^2}\left[1+\left(\frac{1}{1+k}\right)+\left(\frac{1}{1+k}\right)^2+\ldots+\frac{1}{(1+k)^{N-1}}\right]$$

$$= \frac{gS}{(1+k)^2}\left[1-\frac{1}{(1+k)^N}\right]\left[1+\left(\frac{1}{1+k}\right)+\left(\frac{1}{1+k}\right)^2+\ldots\right]$$

$$= \frac{gS}{(1+k)^2}\left[1-\frac{1}{(1+k)^N}\right]\left[\frac{1}{1-\left(\frac{1}{1+k}\right)}\right]$$

$$= \frac{gS}{(1+k)^2}\left[1-\frac{1}{(1+k)^N}\right]\left[\frac{1+k}{k}\right]$$

$$= \frac{gS}{k(1+k)}\left[1-\frac{1}{(1+k)^N}\right]$$

$$= \frac{gS}{k}\left[\frac{1}{(1+k)}-\frac{1}{(1+k)^{N+1}}\right] .$$

For example, when $N = 1$, the growth achieved in the first year leads to a single payment, gS, in the second year that contributes to a present value of

$$\frac{gS}{k(1+k)}\left[1-\frac{1}{(1+k)}\right] = \frac{gS}{(1+k)^2} .$$

By the same reasoning, the second year's growth produces a truncated stream with a present value of

$$\frac{g(1+g)S}{(1+k)^3}\left[1+\frac{1}{(1+k)}+\frac{1}{(1+k)^3}+\dots+\frac{1}{(1+k)^{N-2}}\right]$$

$$=\frac{g(1+g)S}{(1+k)^3}\left[1-\frac{1}{(1+k)^{N-1}}\right]\left[1+\frac{1}{(1+k)}+\frac{1}{(1+k)^2}+\dots\right]$$

$$=\frac{g(1+g)S}{(1+k)^3}\left[1-\frac{1}{(1+k)^{N-1}}\right]\left[\frac{1+k}{k}\right]$$

$$=\frac{g(1+g)S}{k}\left[\frac{1}{(1+k)^2}-\frac{1}{(1+k)^{N+1}}\right].$$

Proceeding in this fashion, the year t's growth results in a present value contribution of

$$Z_t=\frac{g(1+g)^{t-1}S}{k}\left[\frac{1}{(1+k)^t}-\frac{1}{(1+k)^{N+1}}\right]$$

$$=\frac{gS}{k(1+k)}\left[\left(\frac{1+g}{1+k}\right)^{t-1}-\frac{(1+g)^{t-1}}{(1+k)^N}\right].$$

And summing these contributions over the N years of growth, one obtains

$$\sum_{t=1}^{N}Z_t=\frac{gS}{k(1+k)}\left[\sum_{t=1}^{N}\left(\frac{1+g}{1+k}\right)^{t-1}-\sum_{t=1}^{N}\frac{(1+g)^{t-1}}{(1+k)^N}\right]$$

$$=\frac{gS}{k(1+k)}\left\{\left[\frac{1-\left(\frac{1+g}{1+k}\right)^N}{1-\left(\frac{1+g}{1+k}\right)}\right]-\frac{1}{(1+k)^N}\left[\frac{1-(1+g)^N}{1-(1+g)}\right]\right\}$$

$$=\frac{gS}{k}\left\{\left[\frac{1-\left(\frac{1+g}{1+k}\right)^N}{(k-g)}\right]-\frac{1}{(1+k)^{N+1}}\left[\frac{(1+g)^N-1}{g}\right]\right\}.$$

Thus,

$$G' = \frac{\sum_{t=1}^{N} Z_t}{S/k}$$

$$= \left(\frac{g}{k-g}\right)\left[1 - \left(\frac{1+g}{1+k}\right)^N\right] - \left[\frac{(1+g)^N - 1}{(1+k)^{N+1}}\right].$$

On inspection, one can see that this expression corresponds to the earlier year *N* growth factor, less the term

$$\frac{(1+g)^N - 1}{(1+k)^{N+1}}.$$

Because the new sales growth would reach a level of

$$[(1+g)^N - 1]$$

in *N* years, this latter term can be shown to correspond to the present value contribution of the tail of constant "new" sales beyond year *N*.

Appendix C: Total Margin Collapse

In the "total margin collapse," the franchise margin on current business, *fm*, and future business, *(fm)'*, both drop to zero *after* year *N*.

For the "new sales" arising from the sales growth, this is tantamount to the termination of all further sales. But for the initial sales level, the original book value is presumed to provide all necessary capital. Hence, all such sales with a positive margin will contribute some present value. Concentrating at first only on the initial sales component of firm value, let S_0 be the initial sales and m_1 and m_2 represent the margin before and after year *N* of *growth,* which, by our convention, corresponds to the $(N + 1)$ year of sales receipts. We then have the present value

$$m_1 S_0 \left[\frac{1}{1+k} + \frac{1}{(1+k)^2} + \dots + \frac{1}{(1+k)^{N+1}} \right] + m_2 S_0 \left[\frac{1}{(1+k)^{N+2}} + \frac{1}{(1+k)^{N+3}} + \dots \right]$$

$$= \left[m_1 - \frac{k}{T} + \frac{k}{T} \right] S_0 \left[\frac{1}{1+k} + \dots + \frac{1}{(1+k)^{N+1}} \right]$$

$$+ \left[m_2 - \frac{k}{T} + \frac{k}{T} \right] S_0 \left[\frac{1}{(1+k)^{N+2}} + \frac{1}{(1+k)^{N+3}} + \dots \right]$$

$$= \frac{k}{T} S_0 \left[\frac{1}{1+k} + \frac{1}{(1+k)^2} + \dots \right] + \left[m_1 - \frac{k}{T} \right] \frac{S_0}{(1+k)} \left[1 + \frac{1}{(1+k)} + \dots \frac{1}{(1+k)^N} \right]$$

$$+ \left[m_2 - \frac{k}{T} \right] S_0 \left[\frac{1}{(1+k)^{N+2}} + \dots \right]$$

$$= \frac{S_0}{T} + fm_1 \frac{S_0}{k} \left[1 - \left(\frac{1}{1+k} \right)^{N+1} \right] + fm_2 S_0 \left[\frac{1}{(1+k)^{N+2}} + \dots \right]$$

$$= S_0 \left\{ \frac{1}{T} + \frac{fm_1}{k} \left[1 - \left(\frac{1}{1+k} \right)^{N+1} \right] \right\},$$

where

$$fm_1 = m_1 - \frac{k}{T}$$

and by assumption,

$$fm_2 = m_2 - \frac{k}{T}$$

$$= 0 .$$

For the total firm value, we then obtain

$$P = S_0 \left\{ \frac{1}{T} + \frac{fm_1}{k} \left[1 - \left(\frac{1}{1+k} \right)^{N+1} \right] + \frac{(fm)'}{k} G' \right\},$$

where G' has the new margin collapse form derived in Appendix B.

To relate this expression to the illustration depicted in Table 6, the cumulative present value of 7.56 (shown under "Current Sales") corresponds to the factor,

$$\frac{1}{k} \left[1 - \left(\frac{1}{1+k} \right)^{N+1} \right].$$

References

Barbee, William C., Jr., Sandip Mukherji, and Gary A. Raines. 1996. "Do Sales–Price and Debt–Equity Explain Stock Returns Better than Book–Market and Firm Size?" *Financial Analysts Journal*, vol. 52, no. 2 (March/April):56–64.

Bernstein, Peter L. 1956. "Growth Companies vs. Growth Stocks." *Harvard Business Review*, vol. 34, no. 5:87–98.

———. 1996. *Against the Gods*. New York: John Wiley & Sons.

Brown, Stephen J., William N. Goetzmann, and Stephen A. Ross. 1995. "Survival." *Journal of Finance*, vol. 50, no. 3 (July):853–73.

Copeland, Tom, Tim Koller, and Jack Murrin. 1994. *Valuation: Measuring and Managing the Value of Companies*. 2nd ed. New York: John Wiley & Sons.

Damodaran, Aswath. 1994. *Damodaran on Valuation*. New York: John Wiley & Sons.

Fairfield, Patricia M. 1994."P/E, P/B and the Present Value of Future Dividends." *Financial Analysts Journal*, vol. 50, no. 4 (July/August):23–31.

Fisher, Kenneth L. 1984. *Super Stocks*. Woodside, CA: Business Classics.

Fisher, Philip A. 1996. *Common Stocks and Uncommon Profits*. New York: John Wiley & Sons.

Gordon, Myron J. 1962. *The Investment Financing and Valuation of the Corporation*. Homewood, IL: Richard D. Irwin.

Leibowitz, Martin L., and Stanley Kogelman. 1994. *Franchise Value and the Price/Earnings Ratio*. Charlottesville, VA: The Research Foundation of the Institute of Chartered Financial Analysts.

Leibowitz, Martin L., Eric H. Sorensen, Robert D. Arnott, and H. Nicholas Hanson. 1989. "A Total Differential Approach to Equity Duration." *Financial Analysts Journal*, vol. 45, no. 5 (September/October):30–37.

Miller, Merton H., and Franco Modigliani. 1961."Dividend Policy, Growth, and the Valuation of Shares." *Journal of Business*, vol. 34, no. 4 (October):411–33.

Peterson, Pamela P., and David R. Peterson. 1996. *Company Performance and Measures of Value Added*. Charlottesville, VA: The Research Foundation of the Institute of Chartered Financial Analysts.

Rappaport, Alfred. 1986. *Creating Shareholder Value*. New York: The Free Press.

Reilly, Frank K. 1997. *Investment Analysis and Portfolio Management*. 5th ed. Fort Worth, TX: Dryden Press.

Romer, Paul M. 1994. "The Origins of Endogenous Growth." *Journal of Economic Perspectives*, vol. 8 (Winter):3–22.

Smith, Gordon V., and Russell L. Parr. 1994. *Valuation of Intellectual Property and Intangible Assets*. 2nd ed. New York: John Wiley & Sons.

Solnik, Bruno. 1996. *International Investments*. 3rd ed. Reading, MA: Addison-Wesley.

Statman, Meir. 1984. "Growth Opportunities vs. Growth Stocks." *Journal of Portfolio Management*, vol. 10, no. 3 (Spring):70–74.

Stewart, G. Bennett III. 1991. *The Quest for Value*. New York: Harper Business.

Treynor, Jack L. 1972. "The Trouble with Earnings." *Financial Analysts Journal*, vol. 28, no. 5 (September/October):41–43.

———. 1994. "Growth Companies." *Financial Analysts Journal*, vol. 50, no. 6 (November/December):12–16.

Williams, John B. 1938. *The Theory of Investment Value*. Amsterdam: North-Holland Publishing.